Planet in Distress

Joy Brewster

Newbridge®

Before You Read

What do floods, wildfires, droughts, and animal extinction have in common? They can all be effects of global warming. What—or who—is heating up our planet? Humans may have a lot to do with it. But we can do a lot to fix the problem. As you get ready to read this book, think about these questions and make notes.

🌎 Where have you read or heard about global warming and the greenhouse effect?

🌎 In what ways do you think you might be adding to global warming?

Preview the book by looking at the table of contents, headings, photos, and special features.

🌎 What do you see in this book that you already know something about?

🌎 In this book you can get information from photos, a diagram, a chart, and sidebars. Look at the sidebar on page 25. Read the title and look at the photo. How do you think this information will help you understand solutions to global warming?

🌎 List three facts or ideas you think you'll discover in this book.

🌎 What questions do you have about global warming?

Table of Contents

Living on a
Hot Planet

Imagine this: You are a middle schooler living in the United States, 200 years in the future. It is Monday— time to get dressed for school. As usual, rain is drumming nonstop against your windows. It is coming down in sheets. The backyard looks like a lake, and the street looks like a river. You'll have to take the school boat to school again. Last year was different—the **drought** killed all the plants.

Wondering which is worse, you go down to the kitchen, where your family is eating breakfast. You won't be having cereal for breakfast because the drought ruined the grain crops. Storms in other parts of the country have destroyed fruit and vegetable crops, and killed off livestock on farms and ranches. You won't be having juice, fruit, or milk, either.

The Great Flood of 1993 in the Midwest was one of the worst natural disasters ever to hit the United States. Will we have more floods like this in the future?

So what will you eat for breakfast? As you mix bottled water into your powdered breakfast mix, you turn on the TV news. It's not good. Wildfires out west. Floods down south. And off the coast of Maine, another island has been **submerged** by the rising sea.

Finally, the daily animal **extinction** report comes on. It says there are now only four polar bears left in the world—and they live in a zoo. Scientists blame it on the melting **polar ice cap.** You sigh, pull on your boots and rain gear, and stand at the front door to wait for the boat.

Will life in the future really be like this? Could it really happen?

The Temperature Is Going Up... and Up

The things you just read about really could happen. The reason is that our whole planet is getting warmer. Scientists call this **global warming**. They report that temperatures all over the world have risen about one degree Fahrenheit during the last hundred years. And they predict that temperatures could go up another two to ten degrees in the next hundred years.

A degree or two doesn't sound like much. So what if Earth *is* getting warmer? Doesn't that just mean that we won't have to wear heavy winter coats, and we can go swimming all year round?

The trouble is that global warming means more than just warm weather. Even slightly higher temperatures can cause big changes in the natural world. Let's see why some of these weird things you read about could happen in the future.

Global Temperature Change (1880–2000)

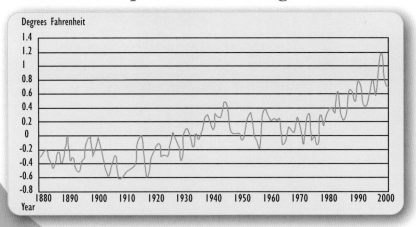

Degrees Fahrenheit

| | 1880 | 1890 | 1900 | 1910 | 1920 | 1930 | 1940 | 1950 | 1960 | 1970 | 1980 | 1990 | 2000 |

Year

Source: U.S. National Climatic Data Center, 2001

6

Why could we have more floods, droughts, storms, and fires?

Scientists believe that global warming will likely cause extremes in weather. The number of extreme rains and huge floods appears to be on the rise.

Engineers design storm sewers, bridges, and other public works to withstand the "hundred-year storm"—that is, the worst flooding that people can expect during a whole century. But Thomas Karl of the National Climatic Data Center pointed out an alarming trend. "There isn't really a hundred-year event anymore . . . we seem to be getting these storms of the century every couple of years."

Drought can ruin a cornfield.

Hurricanes, the greatest storms on earth, could be more powerful in a globally warmed world, producing intense rainfall and disastrous flooding.

A recent study reports that the percentage of Earth's land that suffered serious drought has more than doubled in the last 30 years. Scientists say that almost half of that change is due to rising global temperatures, not decreases in rainfall or snowfall.

Drought can also cause wildfires.

7

Why could some islands be covered by the sea?

Most things expand, or get bigger, when they heat up. As the oceans warm, the water expands and takes up more space. That causes the **sea level** to rise. Sea levels have risen 4–10 inches in the past 100 years. Some scientists predict they could rise another three feet in the next hundred years.

Arctic Ice Cap

EUROPE

ARCTIC OCEAN

ASIA

North Pole

Map Key

— Summer polar ice cap boundary in 1979

— Summer polar ice cap boundary at present

NORTH AMERICA

In the Arctic, more than 20 percent of the polar ice cap has melted since 1979.

Today, the islands of Tuvalu in the South Pacific Ocean are only about six feet above sea level. If sea levels continue to rise, the islands could disappear.

As the ocean rises, it begins to creep up beaches, covering them with water. Sometimes beachfront homes are left standing in the water because there's no beach left—the ocean has gradually risen up and over the old shore.

To make matters worse, huge masses of snow and ice that cover the land at the North and South poles are slowly melting. The melting of these polar ice caps adds water to the world's oceans. In addition, enormous chunks of ice, one the size of Rhode Island, have broken away from ice shelves near the South Pole. **Ice shelves** are large areas of ice that are attached to land, but project out onto the sea. All this melting at the poles makes sea levels rise more and more.

Why could polar bears and other animals be in danger?

In the Arctic, ice on the sea is freezing later and melting earlier each year. That means polar bears are in trouble.

Polar bears hunt on sea ice, fields of ice made of frozen seawater. They catch seals when they come up for air through holes in the ice or rest on the ice. With sea ice freezing later in the fall and melting earlier in the spring, polar bears have less hunting time. That means they have less food to eat each year. No wonder scientists have noticed that polar bears are getting thinner.

A polar bear's big feet let it walk on snow witho[u]t sinking in too much—like snowshoes.

As sea levels rise, salt water could flood the wetlands of the Florida Everglades. This would threaten alligators, which live only in fresh water.

Canvasback ducks migrate north in the summer. As Earth gets warmer, the ducks may adapt by staying up north through the entire year.

Global warming is affecting animal habitats in other places, too. For example, in the American Northwest, fish such as salmon that live in cold water won't be able to **survive** in waters that are too warm.

Living things all over the world depend on a delicate balance of temperature and rainfall in their **habitats.** If the habitats change slowly, species of plants and animals can survive because they have time to adapt over a long period. For example, in a warming world, some animals may stop migrating south in winter. But they will make that change slowly, over many generations and many years.

The trouble with the global warming going on right now is that it is happening too quickly. Plant and animal species don't have time to adapt, so they are dying out. Some scientists believe that more than one million species could become extinct in just 50 years if global warming doesn't slow down.

11

Who Dunnit?
Solving the Mystery of Global Warming

So who's speeding up global warming? The culprits could very well be us. How can that be? To find out, imagine this scene:

Highways are jammed. People are driving to work, to school, to shopping. Cars and trucks sit bumper-to-bumper, or crawl along the road like snails. As their engines burn gas and oil, they send **exhaust fumes** into the air. Those fumes contain **carbon dioxide**—a gas that is one of the main causes of global warming.

Every year, cars and trucks in the United States produce more than a billion tons of carbon dioxide pollution.

The causes of global warming started long ago. Back in 1853, smoke from burning coal poured from a factory in Boston, Massachusetts.

All plants contain carbon, and coal was formed from plants that died millions of years ago. The burning carbon in the coal gives off carbon dioxide. Some coal from the Black Thunder Mine in Wyoming dates from more than 60 million years ago.

But traffic isn't the only cause of global warming. Machines in factories burn coal or oil to make soap, furniture, clothing, car parts—you name it. Power plants burn coal to make electricity. Furnaces burn coal, oil, or natural gas to heat buildings. All these fuels, called **fossil** fuels, release carbon dioxide and other gases into the air when they are burned.

Greenhouse Gases and Global Warming

The Earth is surrounded by gases. We call these gases Earth's atmosphere. Some of the gases are called **greenhouse gases** because they create the **greenhouse effect**. That means they help keep our planet warm enough for people, plants, and animals to live. So far, so good. But when we drive cars and run factories and power plants, we release more of those same gases into the atmosphere. This increases, or enhances, the greenhouse effect and makes temperatures on Earth even warmer.

13

The diagram on the next page shows how the greenhouse effect works. Earth's surface warms as it absorbs sunlight. The Earth's surface also gives off invisible heat energy called **infrared energy.** Greenhouse gases absorb much of this energy. In turn, greenhouse gases give off infrared energy of their own. This creates the greenhouse effect. As greenhouse gases increase, the greenhouse effect also increases.

Planes fly high above the clouds in the atmosphere. You can't see the atmosphere, but life on Earth depends on it.

Most power plants produce energy by burning coal. These plants are the biggest source of carbon dioxide pollution in the United States.

How Greenhouse Gases Warm the Earth

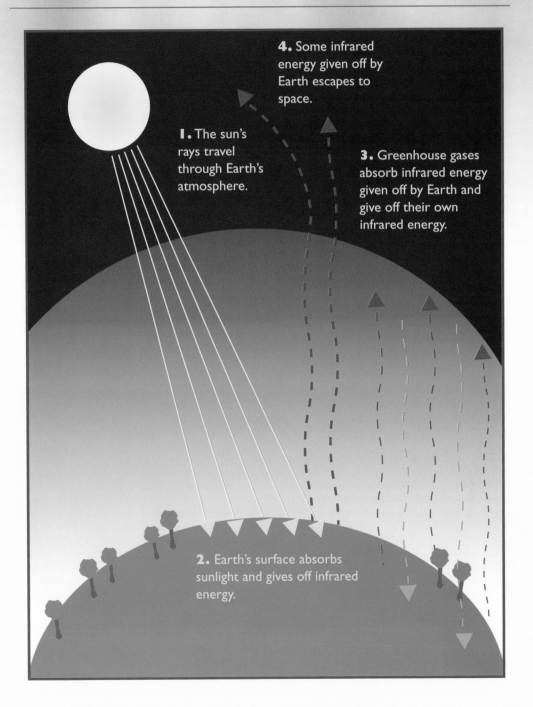

4. Some infrared energy given off by Earth escapes to space.

1. The sun's rays travel through Earth's atmosphere.

3. Greenhouse gases absorb infrared energy given off by Earth and give off their own infrared energy.

2. Earth's surface absorbs sunlight and gives off infrared energy.

Destroying Earth's Forests

Everyone likes trees. They're nice to look at. They give shade on a hot day. They shelter the animals that live high in their branches.

But our leafy friends do much more for the planet. They soak up carbon dioxide from the air and store it in their leaves like giant sponges. This reduces the greenhouse effect by keeping some carbon dioxide from getting into the atmosphere.

So what do we do? While we're burning tons of fuels and pouring carbon dioxide into the air, we're also making things worse by cutting down or burning huge areas of the world's forests. When forests are cut down, there are fewer trees left to soak up carbon dioxide. When trees are burned, it's even worse—all the carbon dioxide they stored in their leaves goes right back into the air.

Some people clear forests to make room for farms and cattle. Others use the wood for building new homes. Whatever the reason, destruction of forests could be another cause of global warming.

Rain forests play an important role in storing Earth's carbon dioxide. But every year, as many as 50 million acres of tropical forests are being destroyed.

Burp! Other Greenhouse Gases

Carbon dioxide isn't the only greenhouse gas humans and animals are adding to the atmosphere. Methane traps even more heat than carbon dioxide. This gas comes from garbage, coal mines, decaying forests, and … cows! Yes, those gentle creatures that give us milk eat a lot of grass. As they digest it, they burp a lot, and, just as we do, they pass gas. That gas is methane, and, with more than a billion cattle worldwide, that's a lot of methane.

Nitrous oxide is another greenhouse gas. It comes from chemical fertilizers. Farmers use fertilizers to help their crops grow. Other people use fertilizer to grow thick green lawns and beautiful flowers.

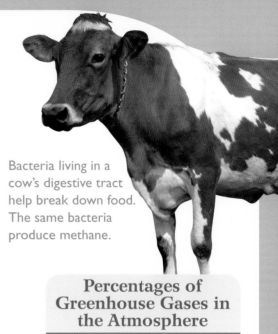

Bacteria living in a cow's digestive tract help break down food. The same bacteria produce methane.

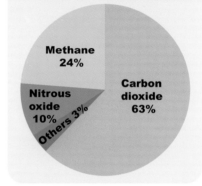

Percentages of Greenhouse Gases in the Atmosphere

Methane 24%

Nitrous oxide 10%

Others 3%

Carbon dioxide 63%

Some forests are burned on purpose to clear land for farming. This "slash-and-burn" practice releases carbon dioxide and methane into the air.

17

Two Views on Global Warming

Most scientists believe that global warming is happening, and that our activities are making it happen faster. But some scientists disagree. They believe that the Earth isn't warming at all, or that the increase in global warming will be so tiny that it won't affect our lives. Reporter Richard Harris talked with two scientists about their different opinions on global warming.

Prof. Richard B. Alley

University of Pennsylvania professor Richard B. Alley believes that humans do contribute to global warming. He is a professor of geosciences—sciences that deal with the Earth.

Professor Alley: You know, it's wonderful what fossil fuels do for us, but they do cause a problem, which is that they're going to change the climate. So the problem now is, can we clean this up before we switch the world into some other mode of behavior that's dangerous?

Mr. Harris: This is not your job as a scientist, to be a social crusader, but is this your job maybe as a dad?

Professor Alley: I certainly hope it will leave [our children] a better world than we've got.... All of us need to look to the future, and I think that we do better by looking ahead, seeing the threats that might be coming, and starting to handle those now.

Dr. John Christy thinks differently. He is a climate scientist and professor at the University of Alabama.

Mr. Harris: … So how much do you think the climate could warm in the next century?

Dr. Christy: It looks like it's on track to warm about one degree Centigrade, one-and-a-half degrees Centigrade—something in that range.

Mr. Harris: Which is about two degrees Fahrenheit, something like that.

Dr. Christy: That's right. At that rate …the human-induced changes are going to be gradual enough that they will be handled by the species we see out there now.

Mr. Harris: You're really challenging the mainstream of thought that climate change is going to be … up to ten degrees Fahrenheit in the next century. … Have you ever asked yourself, 'What if I'm wrong?'

Dr. Christy: … If we do come upon a time of rapid change, I want to be the first to find it, report it in the most precise manner possible so that we can understand what's going on.

Dr. John Christy

How do these two scientists disagree? What do they agree on?

Excerpts from NPR® (National Public Radio) interviews, May 12, 2004 (Prof. Richard B. Alley) and May 13, 2004 (Dr. John Christy). Printed with permission of NPR.

Cool It! Slowing Global Warming

Now you might be saying, "Driving cars, cutting down trees to build houses, raising cows—we can't just stop all those things." And you'd be right. That's exactly why global warming is such a problem. We often harm the environment in order to meet our needs, and yet, without the environment, we have nothing! There must be a solution. Somehow we have to find sources of clean fuel—fuels that don't put more greenhouse gases into the atmosphere. Scientists and engineers are working to do just that. They have already had some success.

This wind farm in California cuts the amount of greenhouse gases by more than a billion pounds each year.

This flying wing runs on solar power. Someday aircraft like this may fly all the way to Mars.

Running on the Wind

Today, on the plains of West Texas, for example, you can see rows of modern-day windmills called wind **turbines.** Each turbine has three giant blades that spin like an airplane propeller. As the blades spin, they turn a machine that makes electricity. Large groups of turbines, called wind farms, can light up whole cities. Unlike power plants, wind farms don't burn fuels that pour greenhouse gases into the air.

Turning in the Tide

In New York City's East River, the changing tide creates strong currents of moving water. These currents will soon turn the blades of turbines that are deep under the water. Like the turbines on wind farms, underwater turbines make electricity. Their big propellers will spin slowly to avoid harming wildlife in the river.

Using Power from the Sun

New York City is building two new subway stations that will be the first ones in the city to use solar power, or power from the sun. The roofs of the stations will be made of special materials that make electricity out of sunlight. The electricity will be used to light up the insides of the stations.

Getting into Hot Water

Deep under the planet's surface, rock is so hot that it melts into liquid. The liquid rock heats up rocks and water that lie under Earth's crust. This heat is called geothermal energy. In some places, water gets so hot that it turns into steam. Pipes carry the steam into power plants where the force of the steam spins turbines, which makes electricity.

Engineers in Boise, Idaho, have found another clever way to use geothermal water. They pump it through a machine that transfers the heat to water that goes into buildings. That way, the city of Boise doesn't have to burn fuel to get hot water to people's homes.

This power plant uses geothermal steam to produce electricity for the city of San Francisco.

Clean-energy power plants like this one in California may soon be a common sight. This plant burns agricultural waste and leftover wood to make electricity.

Putting Garbage to Good Use

Even garbage is becoming a source of energy. Cornstalks, spoiled grain, leftover crops, dead trees, and branches can fuel power plants that make electricity. At the plant, these waste materials are fed into a furnace and burned to boil water and make steam. The steam turns the machines that make electricity. Fuels can also be made from kitchen waste and scrap paper—even manure.

Today waste materials provide only about two percent of our nation's electricity. But they may provide more than half the country's energy by the year 2030.

Once nobody wanted wood chips. Now they are used to make clean fuel—and just about everyone wants that.

It's the Law!

In 2002, California passed the first law in the United States that limits the amount of carbon dioxide that comes from cars. In Chattanooga, Tennessee, buses run on electricity instead of gas. In Dayton, Ohio, police patrol the streets on bikes instead of cars and motorcycles. More and more state and local governments are taking steps to control the amount of greenhouse gases coming from cars and buses. These changes keep tons of carbon dioxide out of the atmosphere.

Driving Cars of the Future—Today!

Imagine a car with a sleek, streamlined design, made of strong, lightweight materials, that travels about twice as far on a gallon of gas as other cars do. This isn't a car of the future—people are driving cars like this today. These new **hybrid** cars have a small gasoline engine that works along with an electric motor. Since the gasoline engine is used only part of the time, it needs about half the gas as the engine on ordinary cars. Hybrid cars are doing more than saving gas—they're cutting down the amount of carbon dioxide going into the air.

This Bus Runs on Veggie Oil

In the summer of 2003, 13 students from Middlebury College in Vermont rattled across the country in an old school bus. Inside and out, their bus smelled like fast-food french fries.

The students had fixed the bus engine so it would run on used vegetable oil instead of diesel oil. They wanted to show people that fuel made from used "veggie oil" was cheap, safe, and clean-burning. And, unlike diesel oil, it was **renewable.** They painted their bus in wild colors, added signs that said, "This Bus Runs on Veggie Oil," and off they went.

Restaurants along the way gave them their used cooking oil, which is why the bus smelled like a fast-food kitchen. But there were no diesel fumes, and the veggie oil was about as cheap as you can get. The group made another trip in 2004. This time they drove a bus that used biodiesel fuel, a fuel that is a mixture of veggie oil, a chemical called lye, and a kind of alcohol. They spent three months on the road promoting cleaner fuels. They called themselves Students for Environmental Awareness. And they called their cause Project Biobus.

Countries Working Together

A new global system will help countries identify problems and better understand Earth's environment. It will also help scientists develop new ways to protect it. Delegates from nearly 60 countries met in Brussels, Belgium, for the 2005 Earth Observation Summit. The nations, including the United States, established a worldwide system that will keep an eye on Earth's environment. Satellites in space and sensing equipment on the ground and in the oceans will track challenges such as climate change and natural disasters.

Delegates to the 2004 Earth Observation Summit met in Tokyo, Japan.

The Kyoto Protocol

In 1997, representatives from more than 100 countries met in Kyoto, Japan, to talk about global warming. They suggested the Kyoto Protocol, an agreement to reduce carbon dioxide **emissions** by five percent by the year 2012. In the following years, many countries signed the agreement. But the United States did not. Some Americans say that the necessary changes would cost jobs and money, and would restrict our way of life. Others argue we can't afford not to participate, since our planet's future is at stake.

Trees for Africa

Nearly 30 years ago, a woman in Africa named Wangari Maathei had a great idea. She was worried about forests that were quickly disappearing in Africa. She started to encourage women in her country, Kenya, to plant trees on their farms. Her work was known as the "Green Belt Movement." Since then, women have planted 30 million trees! In 2004, Wangari Maathai was honored for her work in protecting the forests.

She was the first woman from Africa to receive a great honor called the Nobel Peace Prize. She won the prize "for her contribution to **sustainable** development, democracy, and peace." In the past, she was arrested and put in jail many times for her protests against the destruction of forests. Asked how she was able to be so brave, she said, "…everywhere in the world, people have faced challenges, and they have stood up, and they have taken a lot of risk for what they believed in—people like Martin Luther King [and] Nelson Mandela. It is not my own prize, but a recognition for the entire country."

Living on a Cooler Planet

Remember the beginning of this book, when you imagined that you were living on a hot planet? Now suppose that we humans really do work together to slow down global warming. Here's how that same morning might look:

You are a middle schooler living in the United States, 200 years in the future. It is Monday—time to get dressed for school. The sun fills your room with golden morning light. Outside, the flowers are blooming in nodding crowds of happy colors, and robins are chirping in the apple tree.

Smiling, you head downstairs for the kitchen, where your family is eating breakfast. Your favorite cereal is on the table, along with fresh fruit, orange juice, and milk. You check out the new solar-powered car in the driveway. Some day, you might be driving one. Right now, though, you decide to ride your bike to school— the spring air is sweet, and it seems a perfect way to start the day.

Keep Going!

Now that you've read *Planet in Distress*, use your notes, your smarts, and your research skills to think about this subject in a deeper way. In these activities, you can get answers to questions, meet people who are working to solve the global warming problem, and do your part to help.

THINK AND WRITE

🌍 You read about the Kyoto Protocol. That is the agreement requiring countries to cut emissions of carbon dioxide and other greenhouse gases by 5 percent by the year 2012. The United States did not sign the agreement. Our government's position is that it would cost jobs and money, as well as restrict Americans' way of life. Do you think our country should sign the agreement? Why or why not? Write a persuasive argument expressing your opinion.

DIG AND WRITE

🌍 What questions that you had before you read the book are still unanswered? What new questions came up in reading? Here are some Websites where you can start looking for answers. When you find them, write them down and tell where you found them.

U.S. Environmental Protection Agency Kids Site
www.epa.gov/globalwarming/kids

Global Warming: Early Warning Signs
www.climatehotmap.org

TALK TO THE EXPERTS

🌍 Find out firsthand what scientists, politicians, meteorologists, and others are doing about global warming by interviewing people in these fields. Use resources in your community or Websites to locate specialists. Here is an idea:

• Interview a meteorologist from a local TV or radio station. If possible, meet with him or her at the station. That way, you can see weather maps and other tools that show the effects of global warming.

THINK GLOBALLY, ACT LOCALLY

🌍 You have read about the terrible effects of global warming. You have also learned about actions that people and even whole countries are taking to fight it. Select one important way people can make a difference. Create a diagram, a chart, some computer animation, or any other kind of artwork showing the action. Present it to your class. Explain how this action can help stop global warming.

Glossary

carbon dioxide \kär′ bən dī äk′ sīd \ *n.* a mixture of two gases, carbon and oxygen, that has no color or smell. Animals and humans breathe it out and plants absorb it.

drought \drout\ *n.* a long period of dry weather that ruins crops

emission \ē mi′ shən\ *n.* the discharge or release of a substance such as a chemical or a gas into the atmosphere

exhaust fumes \ig zôst′ fyümz\ *n.* used gases that are released when an engine is running on gasoline or oil

extinction \ik stiŋ′ shən\ *n.* the state of no longer existing

fossil \fä′ səl\ *n.* remains of prehistoric plants or animals that have been preserved in the Earth's crust. Fossil fuels are formed from these remains.

global warming \glō′ bəl wôrm′ iŋ\ *n.* an increase in temperatures on Earth and in the atmosphere

greenhouse effect: \grēn′ hous i fekt′\ *n.* warming of the Earth and its atmosphere by gases that absorb and also give off invisible heat, or infrared, energy

greenhouse gas \grēn′ hous gas\ *n.* a gas in the atmosphere, such as carbon dioxide, that absorbs and also gives off heat, or infrared, energy. Greenhouse gases help keep the Earth-atmosphere system warm enough to sustain life.

habitat \ha′ bə tat\ *n.* the natural environment or place where an animal or plant lives and grows

hybrid \hī′ brəd\ *adj.* coming from two different sources, such as two different plant species

ice shelf \īs′ shelf\ *n.* a very wide and thick sheet of ice that is attached to land on one side. Most of an ice shelf floats on the ocean. Ice shelves are found along the coasts of Antarctica and Greenland.

infrared energy \in frə red′ e′ nər jē\ *n.* invisible energy that becomes heat when it is absorbed by an object

polar ice cap \pō′ lər īs kap′\ *n.* thick cover of ice and snow that blankets the North and South poles

renewable \ri nü′ ə bəl\ *adj.* capable of being renewed. For example, energy that comes from sun, wind, and waves is renewable.

sea level \sē′ le′ vəl\ *n.* the level of the surface of the sea. Sea level is used as a starting point to measure the height or depth of a place: "The mountain peak is 5,000 feet above sea level."

submerge \səb mərj′\ *v.* cover completely with water

survive \sər vīv′\ *v.* continue to live or exist

sustainable \sə stā′ nə bəl\ *adj.* a method of farming or harvesting that does not destroy resources

turbine \tər′ bən\ *n.* an engine that uses gas, water, or air to pass through the blades of a wheel, making them spin

---

Pronunciation Key

\ə\ am**o**ng \ər\ m**ur**der \a\ **a**sk \ā\ **a**pe \ä\ h**o**p, c**a**r \ou\ **ou**t \ch\ **ch**op \e\ **e**nd \ē\ **g**r**ea**sy \g\ **g**et \i\ h**i**d \ī\ **i**ce \j\ **j**et \ŋ\ ki**ng** \ō\ n**o** \ô\ s**aw** \oi\ t**oy** \th\ **th**ank \<u>th</u>\ **th**en \ü\ b**oo**t \oo\ b**oo**k \y\ **y**ou \zh\ A**s**ian

Index